NO LONGER PROPERTY OF
ANYTHINK LIBRARIES/
RANGEVIEW LIBRARY DISTRICT

The Scale of Things

The Scale of
THE SOLAR SYSTEM

Joanna Brundle

Crabtree Publishing Company

www.crabtreebooks.com

CRABTREE
PUBLISHING COMPANY
WWW.CRABTREEBOOKS.COM

Author: Joanna Brundle

Editorial director: Kathy Middleton

Editors: Emilie Dufresne, Janine Deschenes

Design: Jasmine Pointer

Proofreader: Crystal Sikkens

Prepress technician: Tammy McGarr

Print coordinator: Katherine Berti

All facts, statistics, web addresses and URLs in this book were verified as valid and accurate at time of writing.
No responsibility for any changes to external websites or references can be accepted by either the author or publisher.

Image Credits

All images courtesy of Shutterstock.com. With thanks to Getty Images, Thinkstock Photo and iStockphoto.

Background – PremiumArt. Front Cover – AKOMIX water mint. 4–5 – Titov Nikolai, Sunnydream, Sea Owl, robuart. 6–7 – Tetiana Saienko, Sunnydream. 8–9 – Sunnydream. 10–11 – Sunnydream, Fire_Irbis, studioworkstock, KittyVector. 12–13 – Sunnydream, 4zevar, MicroOne. 14–15 – robuart, Sunnydream, Sea Owl. 16–17 – robuart, Sunnydream, 4zevar. 18–19 – Sunnydream, robuart. 20–21 – Sunnydream, Sea Owl. 22–23 – Sunnydream.

Library and Archives Canada Cataloguing in Publication

Title: The scale of the solar system / Joanna Brundle.
Names: Brundle, Joanna, author.
Description: Series statement: The scale of things | Previously published: King's Lynn, Norfolk : BookLife Publishing, 2019. | Includes index.
Identifiers: Canadiana (print) 20190191910 | Canadiana (ebook) 20190191929 |
  ISBN 9780778776581 (hardcover) |
  ISBN 9780778776765 (softcover) |
  ISBN 9781427125309 (HTML)
Subjects: LCSH: Solar system—Juvenile literature. | LCSH: Planets—Juvenile literature. | LCSH: Distances—Measurement—Juvenile literature. | LCSH: Measurement—Juvenile literature. | LCSH: Size perception—Juvenile literature. | LCSH: Size judgment—Juvenile literature.
Classification: LCC QB501.3 .B78 2020 | DDC j523.2—dc23

Library of Congress Cataloging-in-Publication Data

Names: Brundle, Joanna, author.
Title: The scale of the solar system / Joanna Brundle.
Description: New York, New York : Crabtree Publishing Company, 2020. | Series: The scale of things | Includes index.
Identifiers: LCCN 2019043623 (print) | LCCN 2019043624 (ebook) |
  ISBN 9780778776581 (hardcover) |
  ISBN 9780778776765 (paperback) |
  ISBN 9781427125309 (ebook)
Subjects: LCSH: Solar system--Juvenile literature. | Planets--Juvenile literature. | Distances--Measurement--Juvenile literature. | Measurement--Juvenile literature. | Size perception--Juvenile literature. | Size judgment--Juvenile literature.
Classification: LCC QB501.3 .B78 2020 (print) | LCC QB501.3 (ebook) | DDC 523.2--dc23
LC record available at https://lccn.loc.gov/2019043623
LC ebook record available at https://lccn.loc.gov/2019043624

Crabtree Publishing Company

www.crabtreebooks.com   1–800–387–7650

Published by Crabtree Publishing Company in 2020

©2019 BookLife Publishing Ltd.

All rights reserved. No part of this publication may be reproduced, stored in a retrieval system or be transmitted in any form or by any means, electronic, mechanical, photocopying, recording, or otherwise, without the prior written permission of Crabtree Publishing Company.

Printed in the U.S.A./012020/CG20191115

Published in Canada
Crabtree Publishing
616 Welland Ave.
St. Catharines, Ontario
L2M 5V6

Published in the United States
Crabtree Publishing
PMB 59051
350 Fifth Avenue, 59th Floor
New York, New York 10118

CoNTENTS

Page 4	Introduction
Page 6	The Moon and Mercury
Page 8	Mercury and Mars
Page 10	Mars and Venus
Page 12	Venus and Earth
Page 14	Earth and Neptune
Page 16	Neptune and Uranus
Page 18	Uranus and Saturn
Page 20	Saturn and Jupiter
Page 22	Jupiter and the Sun
Page 24	Glossary and Index

Words that are in **bold** can be found in the glossary on page 24.

INTRODUCTION

The scale of things means how one thing compares in size to another. In this book, we will compare objects in our **solar system** by their **diameters** and distances from the Sun.

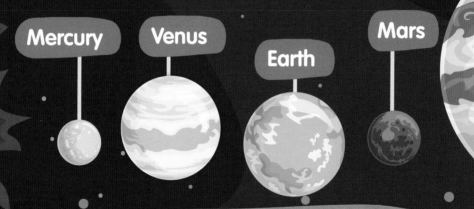

Jupiter

Mercury

Venus

Earth

Mars

Sun

We will measure **the diameters and distances in miles and kilometers (km). The Grand Canyon is up to 18 miles (29 km) across. The greatest distance across the Pacific Ocean, from South America to Asia, is around 12,000 miles (19,312 km). Use these** measurements **to help you imagine the diameters and distances in this book.**

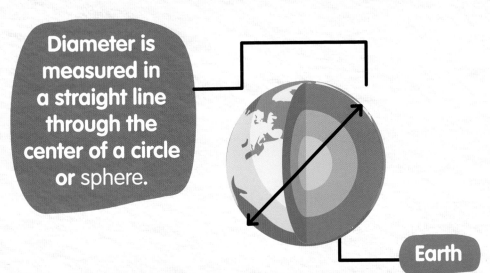

Diameter is measured in a straight line through the center of a circle **or** sphere.

Earth

Uranus

Neptune

Saturn

There are eight planets in our solar system. This picture shows their order from the Sun.

Our solar system is made up of objects such as planets, moons, and stars. They have many different sizes. Some measurements in this book are **approximate**. You can read the measurements that match the ones you learn in school.

THE MOON AND MERCURY

Have you ever seen the Moon in the night sky? It **orbits** our planet, Earth. The diameter of the Moon is 2,160 miles (3,476 km). Earth's diameter is 7,918 miles (12,742 km).

7,918 miles
(12,742 km)

Earth

Moon

2,160 miles
(3,476 km)

The distance between the Moon and Earth is 238,855 miles (384,400 km). That's about 30 TIMES the diameter of Earth.

Moon

Mercury is the smallest planet in our solar system. Its diameter is 3,032 miles (4,880 km). That's almost **ONE AND A HALF TIMES** bigger than the Moon's diameter.

3,032 miles (4,880 km)

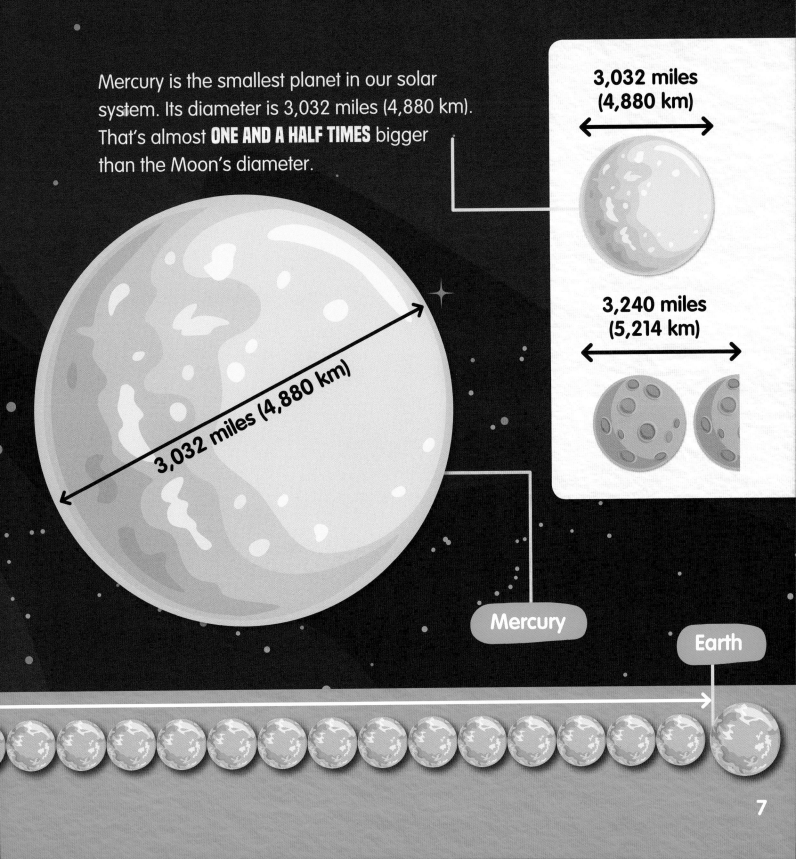

**3,032 miles
(4,880 km)**

**3,240 miles
(5,214 km)**

Mercury

Earth

MERCURY AND MARS

In our solar system, Mercury is the closest planet to the Sun.

The Sun

The distance from Mercury to the Sun is less than half of the distance from Earth to the Sun.

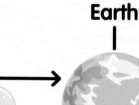

Earth

Mercury

4,212 miles (6,779 km)

4,320 miles (6,952 km)

Mars is the second smallest planet. Its diameter is 4,212 miles (6,779 km). That's 1,180 miles (1,900 km) bigger than Mercury. Mars's diameter is almost **TWICE** as big as the Moon's.

The Moon

Mars

Mercury

4,212 miles (6,779 km)

MARS AND VENUS

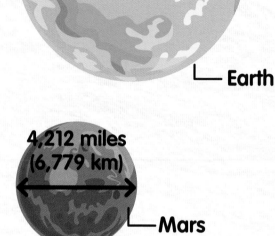

7,918 miles
(12,742 km)
└ Earth

4,212 miles
(6,779 km)
└ Mars

Mars is called the Red Planet because of its reddish color. It is the fourth planet from the Sun. **Scientists** have sent **spacecraft** to Mars to learn more about the planet.

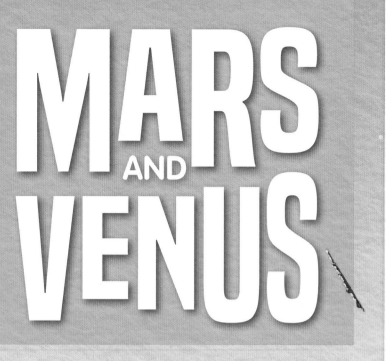

The diameter of Mars is a little more than half the diameter of Earth.

Robotic spacecraft on Mars

Venus is the second planet from the Sun, and the third-smallest in size. Its diameter is 7,521 miles (12,104 km). That's bigger than the diameters of Mars and Mercury, added together.

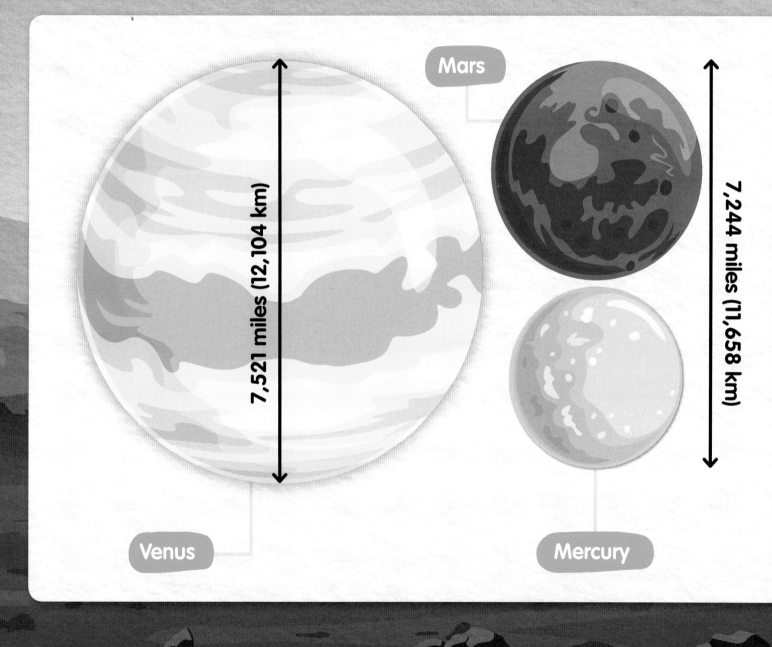

Mars

Venus

Mercury

7,521 miles (12,104 km)

7,244 miles (11,658 km)

VENUS AND EARTH

7,521 miles (12,104 km)

Venus

7,918 miles (12,742 km)

Earth

Venus is the second planet from the Sun. Even though Mercury is closer to the Sun, Venus is the hottest planet in the solar system! It is also the closest planet to Earth

Earth is the fourth-smallest planet in our solar system. With a diameter of 7,918 miles (12,742 km), Earth is just slightly bigger than Venus. It is also the third planet from the Sun.

The Sun

Mercury

93 million miles (150 million km)

Earth is around 93 million miles (150 million km) from the Sun. If you could fly this distance in an airplane, the journey would take around 20 years.

EARTH AND NEPTUNE

Earth orbits the Sun. It takes just over one year, or 365 days and one-quarter of a day, for Earth to move all the way around the Sun.

The Sun

Earth

Earth is the only planet on which we know there are living things.

Neptune is the fifth-smallest planet. Its diameter is around 30,599 miles (49,244 km). This is almost **FOUR TIMES** bigger than Earth's diameter, and **14 TIMES** bigger than the Moon's.

Neptune

30,599 miles (49,244 km)

31,672 miles (50,971 km)

30,599 miles (49,244 km)

30,240 miles (48,667 km)

Earth

Neptune

Moon

NEPTUNE AND URANUS

Neptune is made up of ice, water, and **gas**. On **average**, it is the coldest planet in the solar system and is very windy. Neptune is also the farthest planet from the Sun.

Neptune

The distance from Neptune to the Sun is **30 TIMES** the distance from the Earth to the Sun.

The Sun

Earth

2.8 billion miles (4.5 billion km)

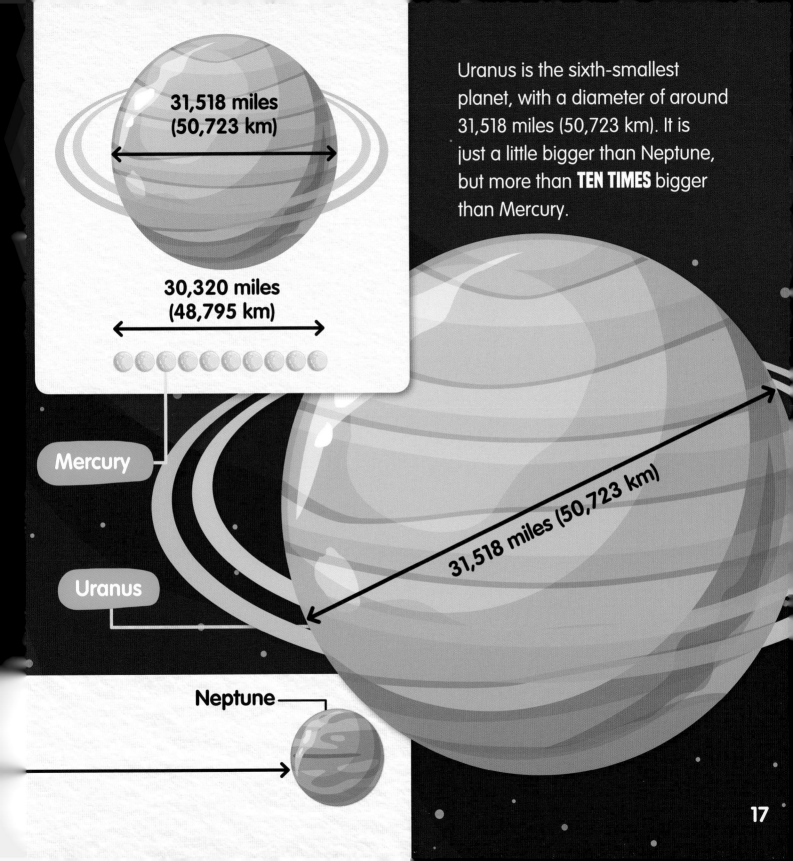

31,518 miles
(50,723 km)

30,320 miles
(48,795 km)

Mercury

Uranus

Neptune

31,518 miles (50,723 km)

Uranus is the sixth-smallest planet, with a diameter of around 31,518 miles (50,723 km). It is just a little bigger than Neptune, but more than **TEN TIMES** bigger than Mercury.

URANUS
AND
SATURN

Uranus is the seventh planet from the Sun. It is around 1.8 billion miles (2.9 billion km) away. That is around **19 TIMES** farther than the distance from Earth to the Sun.

Uranus

There are 27 different moons that orbit Uranus.

Saturn is the second-biggest planet in our solar system. Its diameter is around 74,898 miles (120,536 km). That's over **TWICE** the diameter of Uranus and **NINE TIMES** the diameter of Earth.

Saturn

74,898 miles (120,536 km)

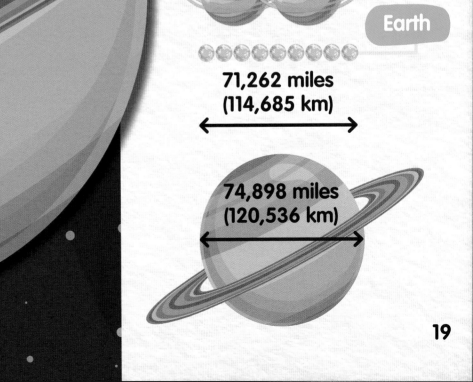

63,036 miles
(101,448 km)

Earth

71,262 miles
(114,685 km)

74,898 miles
(120,536 km)

SATURN AND JUPITER

Saturn is the sixth planet from the Sun. The distance from Saturn to the Sun is around 886 million miles (1.4 billion km). That is around half the distance from Uranus to the Sun.

Saturn

Saturn is made of different gases. Its rings are made of ice, rock, and dust.

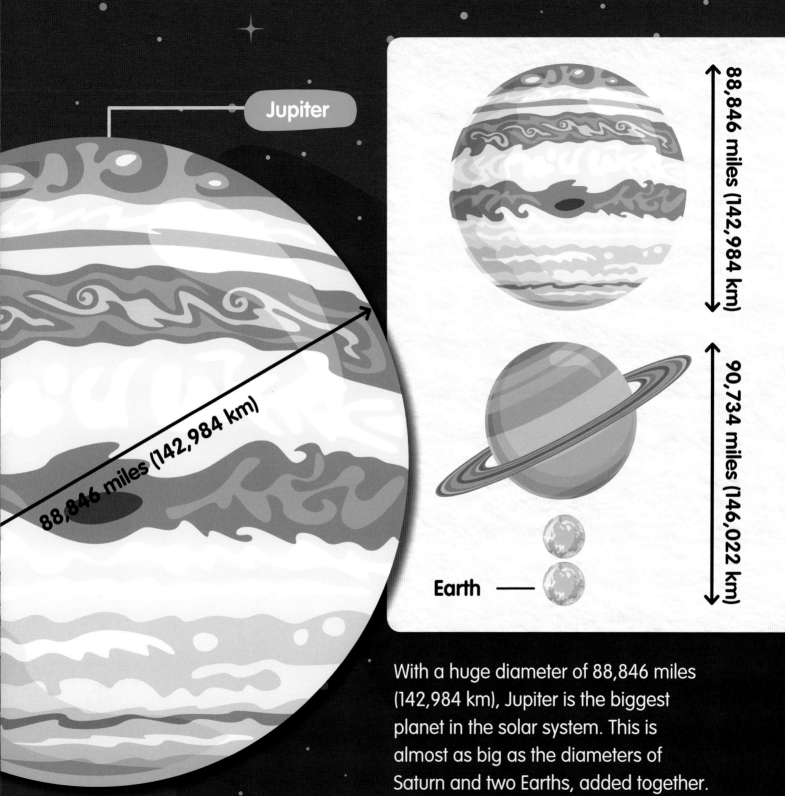

Jupiter

88,846 miles (142,984 km)

88,846 miles (142,984 km)

90,734 miles (146,022 km)

Earth

With a huge diameter of 88,846 miles (142,984 km), Jupiter is the biggest planet in the solar system. This is almost as big as the diameters of Saturn and two Earths, added together.

JUPITER AND THE SUN

Jupiter is the fifth planet from the Sun. On its **surface** is a giant spot, called the Great Red Spot. The spot is actually a huge storm that has been going on for hundreds of years.

Earth

The Great Red Spot is slowly getting smaller. At one time, it was **FOUR TIMES** the diameter of Earth.

The Great Red Spot

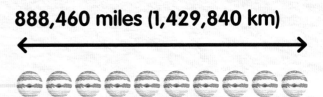

888,460 miles (1,429,840 km)

The Sun

864,336 miles (1,391,014 km)

Jupiter is the largest planet, but the Sun is much bigger. The Sun's diameter is 864,336 miles (1,391,014 km). That is almost **TEN TIMES** the diameter of Jupiter, and more than **100 TIMES** the diameter of Earth.

GLOSSARY

approximate Close to an exact measurement

average A usual amount

diameter An imaginary straight line that passes through the center of a circle or sphere, from one side to the other

gas Substances, such as air, that are not liquids or solids and do not have a fixed shape

measure Find out the size or amount of something

measurements The numbers we get after measuring things

orbits Moves in a curved path around something

scientists People who study and have a lot of knowledge about a type of science

solar system A star with a group of space objects that orbit around it. Our solar system is made up of our Sun, eight planets, and other objects such as moons.

spacecraft Vehicles or machines that are used for exploring space

sphere A globe-shaped object

surface The outside of an object

INDEX

Earth 4–6, 8, 10, 12–16, 18–19, 21–23
Great Red Spot 22
Jupiter 21–23
Mars 9–11
Mercury 7–9, 11, 17

Moon 6–7, 9, 15
moons 5, 18, 22
Neptune 14–17
rings 20
Saturn 19–21
spacecraft 10

Sun 4–5, 8, 12–14, 16, 18, 20, 23
Uranus 17–20
Venus 11–13